KT-133-715

DAVID R. CLARK

«THAT BLACK DAY»
THE MANUSCRIPTS OF
'CRAZY JANE ON THE DAY OF JUDGEMENT'

NEW YEATS PAPERS XVIII

THE DOLMEN PRESS
in association with HUMANITIES PRESS INC.

CONTENTS

General Editor: Liam Miller

Copyright © David R. Clark 1980
Yeats quotations, unpublished manuscripts and photographs of
manuscripts copyright © Anne Yeats and Michael Butler Yeats 1980

Set in Baskerville type and printed in the Republic of Ireland
Printers for the publishers,

DOLMEN PRESS
The Lodge, Mountrath, Portlaoise, Ireland.

North America: Humanities Press Inc.
Atlantic Highlands, New Jersey 07716, USA

First published 1980

BRITISH LIBRARY CATALOGUING IN PUBLICATION DATA
Clark, David Ridgley
     'That black day'. — (New Yeats papers; 18)
     1. Yeats, William Butler. Crazy Jane on the
        day of Judgement
     2. Yeats, William Butler — Criticism, Textual
     I. Title   II. Series
     821'8   PR5904.C7
     ISBN 0-85105-355-6

     ISBN 0 85105 355 6   The Dolmen Press
     ISBN 0 391 02149 4   Humanities Press Inc.

For Jack Nielsen
— my first friend in Ireland —
who welcomed me to Ireland in 1957,
and in whose home — "Castlefield," Clondalkin —
this essay was finished in 1978,
a few months before his sudden and untimely death.

THAT BLACK DAY: THE MANUSCRIPTS OF CRAZY JANE ON THE DAY OF JUDGEMENT'

I

"Supreme art," wrote W. B. Yeats, "is a traditional statement of certain heroic and religious truths, passed on from age to age, modified by individual genius, but never abandoned."[1] It is a critical commonplace that the best art is both traditional and unique.

It is another critical commonplace that W. B. Yeats's own work quite regularly lives up to the standard set in this sentence which he wrote in a 1909 diary and published in his autobiography many years later.

Moreover, with the publication of more and more of Yeats's manuscripts, readers are becoming aware that for many poems and plays a nearly complete record exists of the evolutionary process by which "a traditional statement of certain heroic and religious truths" was "modified by [Yeats's] individual genius" to become "supreme art."

"Genius" is, of course, the key word. Though the mountains of manuscript revisions of *The Countess Cathleen, The Shadowy Waters, Deirdre,* and *The Player Queen* demonstrate that genius, particularly in Yeats's case, was one per cent inspiration, ninety-nine per cent perspiration, they also demonstrate that the one per cent was necessary and was there. At certain crucial points of the evolutionary development the manuscripts often show what may better be called saltations—sudden jumps that could not have been foretold from previous manuscripts. And it is often these very saltations that make the difference between a verse exercise—imitative and derivative—and a true work of art—finished and unique. Writers may learn much about the art of creative revision from a study of Yeats's manuscripts. But often the jump from earlier manuscripts to a near-final version teaches us nothing, merely inspires awe. The earlier manuscripts (as Blake said of Swedenborg's writings) are "the linen clothes folded up."[2]

It often happens too that the saltation by which the poem reaches its unique, nearly finished form also takes it out of the realm of easy comprehensibility. The early drafts may contain clear statement of a logically developed thought. The final draft often boggles the mind—thrills, it, astonishes it, but fails to comfort it with a reasonable answer. "Man can embody truth but he cannot know it," said Yeats in an often quoted letter. "You can refute Hegel but not the Saint or the Song of Sixpence."[3] It is natural to turn to Yeats's manuscripts for light on obscure passages in his poems, and we have an obligation to do this, since the manuscripts exist. But an early manuscript can not tell us what a poem means, only what it once meant. It can only suggest the process the poem went through. The saltation by which the poem became a work of art probably also took it out of the reach of analysis as thought. The eagle of genius carries the viper of reason aloft from its familiar ground. It is fascinating to see this happening in the record of the poem's creation. We learn something about the way the mind works. But we find no "explanation" of the poem.

In this essay I shall look at the manuscripts of one small poem, "Crazy Jane on the Day of Judgment," for evidence of "traditional statement" on the one hand, and, on the other, the "modification by individual genius" which turns that traditional thought into irrefutable song.

'Love is all
Unsatisfied
That cannot take the whole
Body and soul';
And that is what Jane said.

'Take the sour
If you take me,
I can scoff and lour
And scold for an hour.'
'That's certainly the case,' said he.

'Naked I lay,
The grass my bed;
Naked and hidden away,
That black day';
And that is what Jane said.

'What can be shown?
What true love be?
All could be known or shown
If Time were but gone.'
'That's certainly the case,' said he.[4]

"Crazy Jane on the Day of Judgment" is third in a series of twenty-five poems called "Words for Music Perhaps" in one of Yeats's greatest volumes of poetry, *The Winding Stair* (1933). Crazy Jane is the speaker in seven of the poems in the series. The irrefutable quality of the Song of Sixpence rather than of the Saint is what Yeats aimed at in these poems. Crazy Jane is no saint. Whereas in the austere *The Tower* (1928), the old poet, faced with "dull decrepitude," had determined to "make [his] soul" so that "Once out of nature" he need never take his "bodily form from any natural thing" (*Variorum Poems,* pp.416, 408), in *The Winding Stair* he turns back into life, celebrates the rebirth of Self, is content "to live it all again/And yet again" (*Variorum Poems,* p.479) choosing "rebirth rather than deliverance from birth" (*Letters,* p.729).

He cites *(Variorum Poems*, p. 831) his spring 1929 health: "Life returned to me as an impression of the uncontrollable energy and daring of the great creators; it seemed to me that but for journalism and criticism, all that evasion and explanation, the world would be torn in pieces." It was "in memory of those exultant weeks" that he chose the title "Words for Music Perhaps." These poems were to be "all emotion and all impersonal" *(Letters,* p. 758). "Sexual abstinence fed their fire," he wrote. "I was ill and yet full of desire. They sometimes came out of the greatest mental excitement I am capable of " *(Letters,* p.814).

Yeats tells us that Crazy Jane "is more or less founded upon an old woman who lives in a little cottage near Gort. She loves her flower-garden. . .and [has] an amazing power of audacious speech. One of her great performances is a description of how the meanness of a Gort shopkeeper's wife over the price of a glass of porter made her so despair of the human race that she got drunk. The incidents of that drunkenness are of an epic magnificence. She is the local satirist and a really terrible one" *(Letters,* pp. 785-6).

It is probably just as well for Yeats that Crazy Jane, or Cracked Mary as she was actually called, never saw the words Yeats puts into her mouth. As Yeats presents her, she curses the Bishop, tells how Jack the Journeyman had her virginity, how she leaves the door unlatched to him, how her body is "like a road/That men pass over," how she embraces foul as well as fair because "Love has pitched his mansion in/The place of excrement," how she exalts her youth when she had the limbs to try the dance of love however violent *(Variorum Poems,* pp. 507-15).

Yet these poems cannot stay in the realm of the physical; they inevitably are concerned with the metaphysical as well. Physical love is at war with time and old age. Can love survive youth, health, strength, life itself? Moreover, yearning is infinite, whereas physical satisfaction is finite. Can love express itself fully by means of the body, even in youth? These poems go through physical experience and beyond it. They celebrate physical love and meet the problem of time not by talking about reincarnation, living it all again, but by affirming a metaphysical reality:

'Whatever stands in field or flood,
Bird, beast, fish or man,
Mare or stallion, cock or hen,
Stands in God's unchanging eye
In all the vigour of its blood;
In that faith I live or die' *(Variorum Poems,* p. 529).

Before turning to the manuscripts we must review a relevant bit of what had been "passed on from age to age" to Yeats before he wrote this little poem on the nature of love. An important idea in the poem, and in Yeats's thought generally, relates to the definition of love ascribed to Aristophanes in Plato's *Symposium.*

". . .Human nature was originally one and we were a whole, and the desire and pursuit of the whole is called love." Yeats was able to make serious use of the details of Aristophanes' speech. ". . . The primeval man was round, his back and sides forming a circle; and he had four hands and the same number of feet, one head with two faces, looking opposite ways, set on a round neck and precisely alike...." "Terrible was [the] might and strength" of these human creatures so that a worried Zeus said, " 'I will cut them in two and then they will be diminished in strength' "; and he did so, "as you might divide an egg with a hair."[5]

Stephen Winnett in his edition of the manuscripts of *The Only Jealousy of Emer,* which Yeats was writing in 1917, points out a hitherto unnoticed adaptation of this parable:

Woman of the Sidhe   Have you not heard that man before his birth
Is two in one: the yoke & white of the egg
And that one half is born in wretchedness
While the other half remains amid the Sidhe

Cuchulain   I have heard the learned say so

Woman of Sidhe   And have they told you
That the half born into the flesh must seek
For the half it could but find among the Sidhe
In women that are its image in a glass
And loves the more the closer they resemble
Its separated half.

This interpretation is a bit too transcendental for Cuchulain as it would have been for Crazy Jane.

Cuchulain   The learned say so
Because they have understanding & no bowels
For what can understanding know of life....

Woman of the Sidhe   You have sought perfection & to every man
There can be nothing perfect but that half
That hovers amid the Sidhe....

....

Cuchulain   You never can have loved unless you know
It's the imperfect that we love....[6]

10

In later uses Yeats is truer to Aristophanes' parable; couples seek oneness, rather than perfection, but oneness cannot be found in the time-bound world, though sexual congress can give an image of it.

Yeats used Plato's tale of whole and divided humanity in the 1925 *A Vision* to illustrate the nature of the universe and of man and woman in eternity and time. "I see the Lunar and Solar cones first, before they start their whirling movement, as two worlds lying one within another—nothing exterior, nothing interior, Sun in Moon and Moon in Sun—a single being like man and woman in Plato's Myth, and then a separation and a whirling for countless ages, and I see man and woman as reflecting the greater movement."[7] He had used the tale again in the poem "Summer and Spring" (1926). The speaker and his sweetheart "Knew that we'd halved a soul/And fell the one in t'other's arms/That we might make it whole. . ." (*Variorum Poems*, pp. 456–57).

But his most noted use of Plato's tale was in "Among School Children" (1927). Maud Gonne, recalling her childhood,

> Told of a harsh reproof, or trivial event
> That changed some childish day to tragedy—
> Told, and it seemed that our two natures blent
> Into a sphere from youthful sympathy,
> Or else, to alter Plato's parable,
> Into the yolk and white of the one shell
>
> *(Variorum Poems,* p. 443).

In Yeats's system a man loves a woman wholly and as she is specifically because she is his opposite and complement. He longs for "whole" to be "joined to whole" (*Variorum Poems*, p. 555). "The ultimate reality because neither one nor many, concord nor discord, is symbolized as a phaseless sphere ["our two natures blent/Into a sphere"—] but...all things fall into a series of antinomies in human experience...."[8] "... The natural union of man and woman has a kind of sacredness" as "a symbol of that eternal instant where the antinomy is resolved" (*A Vision,* 1937, p. 214). "Love is created and preserved by intellectual analysis, for we love only that which is unique, and it belongs to contemplation not to action, for we would not change that which we love. A lover will admit a greater beauty that that of his mistress but not its like, and surrenders his days to a delighted laborious study of all her ways.... Fragment delights in fragment and seeks possession . . ."(*A Vision,* 1925, p. 187). Sometimes Yeats's relation with Maud Gonne approximated these states of wholeness or division. "I thought we became one in a world of emotion eternalized by its own intensity and purity...."[9] Donald Torchiana points out that the lines in *Among School Children* about the sphere and the egg may come not only from "Plato's parable," and from the Leda myth, but also from Maud Gonne's designs for the story of the Children of Lir and their trans-

11

formation into swans: "a sphere containing two swans intertwined, ultimately blent as one, an obvious symbol of kindred souls."[10]

As we shall see, Crazy Jane puts impossible demands on physical contact. Her yearning is for that state of "two worlds lying one within another—nothing exterior, nothing interior" (*A Vision*, 1925, p. 149). Her desire is obviously not merely physical but metaphysical. She wants for herself and Jack the Journeyman the sort of union which four years later Yeats gave to another set of fictional lovers, fortunate enough to be made immortal.

One of the abandoned drafts of "Crazy Jane on the Day of Judgment" is perhaps the germ of "Ribh at the Tomb of Baile and Aillinn." The latter were lovers who died for each other and were reunited in the spirit world by Aengus, the Celtic God of Love. Ribh the hermit uses the light cast by the reunited spirits as a sort of bridge lamp by which to read his holy book.

> The miracle that gave them such a death
> Transfigured to pure substance what had once
> Been bone and sinew; when such bodies join
> There is no touching here, not touching there,
> Nor straining joy, but whole is joined to whole;
> For the intercourse of angels is a light
> Where for its moment both seem lost, consumed
>
> *(Variorum Poems*, p. 555).

Crazy Jane's longing for ultimate contact is doomed to disappointment. Although, Yeats says, "the natural union of man and woman... [is] a symbol of that eternal instant where the antinomy is resolved," nevertheless "It is not the resolution itself. There is a passage in Lucretius translated by Dryden. . .which is quite conclusive" (*A Vision*, 1937, p. 214). Lucretius, Book IV, "On the Nature of Love," is perhaps the passage Yeats refers to. Its theme is the inability of love to satisfy by physical contact its infinite desire for union.

> So love with phantoms cheats our longing eyes,
> Which hourly seeing never satisfies:
> Our hands pull nothing from the parts they strain,
> But wander o'er the lovely limbs in vain.
> Nor when the youthful pair more closely join,
> When hands in hands they lock, and thighs in thighs
>   they twine,
> Just in the raging foam of full desire,
> When both press on, both murmur, both expire,
> They gripe, they squeeze, their humid tongues they
>   dart,
> As each would force their way to t'other's heart:
> In vain; they only cruise about the coast;

12

The Reunion of the Soul & the Body

London, Published May 1 1808 by R. H. Cromek, 64 Strand

For bodies cannot pierce, nor be in bodies lost,
As sure they strive to be, when both engage
In that tumultuous momentary rage....[11]

The intercourse of angels is something else again, as the Archangel
Raphael has explained to Adam:

Whatever pure thou in the body enjoy'st
(And pure thou wert created) we enjoy
In eminence, and obstacle find none
Of membrane, joynt, or limb, exclusive barrs:
Easier then Air with Air, if Spirits embrace,
Total they mix, Union of Pure with Pure
Desiring; nor restrain'd conveyance need
As Flesh to mix with Flesh, or Soul with Soul
(*Paradise Lost,* VIII: 622–29).[12]

Swedenborg according to Yeats had described "that marriage of the
angels. . .as a contact of the whole being" *(Autobiography,* p. 164) or
as "a conflagration of the whole being" (*Letters,* p. 805). It may be,
however, that after death Crazy Jane may find the ideal love-making
she desires. The dead, according to Yeats, "make love in that union
which Swedenborg has said is of the whole body and seems from far off
an incandescence."[13] Yeats was, of course, saturated in William Blake's
ideas, and part of the context of this desire for perfect contact may be
Blake's saying that "Embraces are Cominglings from the Head even to
the Feet,/And not a pompous High Priest entering by a Secret Place"
(Jerusalem 69: 43-4). Certainly the lines "Those lovers, purified by
tragedy/Hurry into each others arms" in the Ribh poem might have
been suggested by Blake's illustration "The Reunion of Soul and Body"
for Blair's *The Grave.* Yeats had described the engraving—"We see the
body and soul rushing into each other's arms at the last day,"[14] —and
his description echoes Fuseli's note: ". . .They rush together with
inconceivable energy; they meet, never again to part!"[15] Yeats adds
"their union is. . .that final peace of God wherein body and soul cry
'hither' with one voice" (*The Poems of William Blake,* p. xlv). In
Blakean terms "The Emanation" or "feminine side which, though sub-
merged during the life in this world, operates as man's inspiration. . .
ultimately emerges and joins the spiritual body when the complete
individual has attained Eternity."[16] Yeats understood Spectre and
Emanation to be Blake's "technical expression for reason and emotion,
active and passive, masculine and feminine, past and future, body and
soul, and all the other duads of his complex system" (*The Poems of
William Blake.* p. 249).
    I cannot believe that Yeats did not also think of "The Whirlwind of
Lovers," Blake's illustration of the Paolo and Francesca episode in
Dante's *Inferno.* The lovers are shown twice, once in the huge flame

Plate 2: "The Whirlwind of Lovers." *Inferno*, Canto V. Watercolour.

rising from the form of the swooned Dante and once kissing in the sun above Virgil's head. Albert S. Roe explains that "Paolo and Francesca in the flame may be thought of as the poet's spectre and emanation, the Dante and Beatrice of this world, who will become one again when the sleeping humanity of Dante awakens at the end of his mortal life and re-enters Eden. Linked to Dante through the person of Virgil, his Divine Imagination, is the sun—symbol of Eden, of Los, and of the never-failing joy of God's boundless love and endless mercy. It dominates the scene and in the very center of its disk is shown the instant when, at the moment of entry into Eden, the spectre and emanation reunite to become the Eternal Humanity."[17]

In the flame Paolo and Francesca are time-bound contraries floating together in a sort of balanced dance of attraction and repulsion. Their separate bodies are distinct. In the sun they are so united that it is hard for the viewer's eye to distinguish their separate members. One arm could belong to either person. Their union is an incandescence as in Swedenborg and sheds such a light as that by which Ribh reads his holy book. When Yeats wrote of himself and Maud Gonne that "our two

15

Plate 3: "The Whirlwind of Lovers." *Inferno*, Canto V. Engraving.

natures blent/Into a sphere from youthful sympathy" he may have thought of this sphere as well as of the sphere in which Maud Gonne unites the children of Lir in the form of swans. If we read again a passage already quoted from *A Vision* this picture may give it added suggestion:

> I see the Lunar and Solar cones first, before they start their whirling movement, as two worlds lying one within another—nothing exterior, nothing interior. . .a single being like man and woman in Plato's Myth, and then a separation and whirling for countless ages, and I see man and woman as reflecting the greater movement. . .and all whirling perpetually *(A Vision,* 1925, p. 149).

These two states—the single being and the separated beings—are represented by the two images of Paolo and Francesca, one united in the sun, the other as separated and whirling. The condition of Paolo and Francesca in the flame is the condition in which Jane finds herself and Jack. The condition of Paolo and Francesca in the sphere is the condition to which Jane aspires.

16

Let us turn to the manuscripts, though I shall bring in other items from the intellectual context of the poem as these items are pointed to by specific lines.

On the right-hand page of a notebook begun in Dublin in August 1929 Yeats wrote the prose Draft 1. (See overleaf. Square brackets contain editorial additions to the manuscript. Braces indicate an overwriting as in $\begin{smallmatrix}J\\F\end{smallmatrix}$ or sometimes an added letter or punctuation mark. An asterisk indicates an undeciphered letter. Cancellations, slightly conventionalized, imitate those in the manuscript.)[18]

There is no evidence that Judgment Day had any part in this original idea. The prose sketch centers on knowing—in both the sexual and the intellectual senses. Though Jane has a listener, the poem is her monologue. Jack, if it is her lover Jack the Journeyman, is wordless, if not speechless! The three things Jane asks are: (1) Tell me all, (2) take me all as I am, the bad with the good, and (3) touch me all over. Love for the whole of Jack's soul is Jane's aim in Stanza 1. To that end she demands to hear all her lover's history. Her aim in Stanza 2 is that the whole of her own soul be loved. To that end she demands that Jack accept her unkindness as a necessary part of her. In Stanza 3 it is the whole of her body that she wants loved. She demands that he "touch all portions" and not miss one. Earthy as this sketch is, its theme is Platonic. Each stanza demonstrates Aristophanes' thought that "Love is the desire and pursuit of the whole," or, as the refrain puts it, that "Love is for wholes whether of body or souls Etc." The first stanza of the printed poem emerges from this refrain:

> 'Love is all
> Unsatisfied
> That cannot take the whole
> Body and soul'. . . .

The movement of this prose sketch is toward body rather than soul, the third stanza being climactically and exclusively physical. Yet this excessive physicality is self-frustrating. Only spirits or angels can make love that thoroughly. Such love is not for men and women bound to time and flesh.

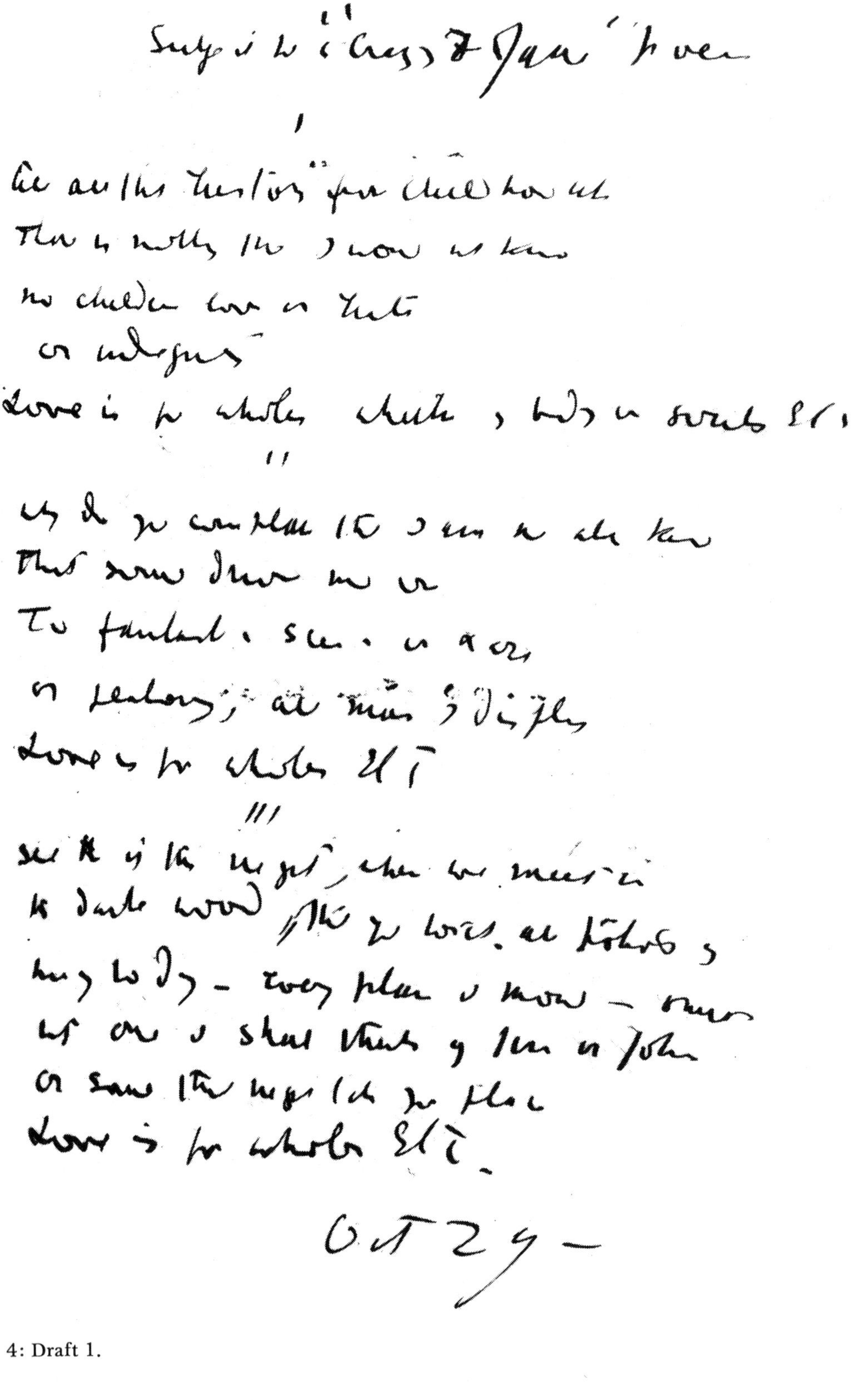

*Draft 1

I

Subject for a 'Crazy F.$^{J?}$ Jane' Poem

I

Tell all that history from childhood up

There is nothing that I would not know

No childe* love or hate

or indignity

Love is for wholes whether of body or souls Etc

II

Why do you complain that I am not always kind

That some[thing] drives me on

To fantastic scenes on & on

or jealousy, all mus[t] I display

Love is for wholes Etc

III

See ~~th~~ in the night, when we meet in

the dark wood ,, that you touch all potions of

my body—every plane & mound—omit

but one I shall think of Jim or John

or some that might take your place

Love is for wholes Etc.

Oct 29—

19

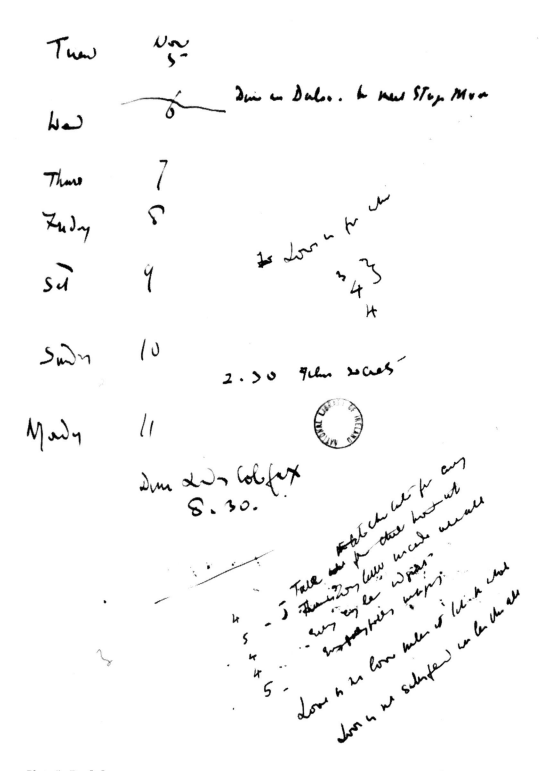

Plate 5: Draft 2.

Draft 2 occupies part of a left hand page facing Draft 1. Some notes and numbers are jotted down with no attempt at legibility.

Draft 2

```
  Fo   Love is for who


            3 ⌐
                ⌐
            4 ⌐


            4



        1⌐   the tale whole tale for every
  4     Tale  all from child hood up


  5     There is Every little incide[nt] all all


  4
        Every every le[ast] indgint [?=indignity?]
  4

  5     Every folly folly in *****


     Love is not love unless it take the whol[e]


     Love is not satisfied with less than all
```

Note: The bracket joining 3 and 4 is Yeats's.

The poet is sketching the verse form, and the numbers indicate the beats per line. Yeats first thought of longer lines than those he finally settled on. The lines in the completed poem have a 3/4 or 3/5 alternation. Here he has two completed five-beat lines (which were perhaps meant to fit into the scheme 45445). The unfinished lines do not fit the numbers beside them. Certain rhyme words—"all," "whole" —and the long e sound in the endings of the rhymes "every" and "indignity," remain in the finished poem. This draft, however, does not achieve a rhyme scheme.

The five-beat lines are refinements of the refrain used in the prose sketch. "Love is for wholes whether of body or souls." Yeats still

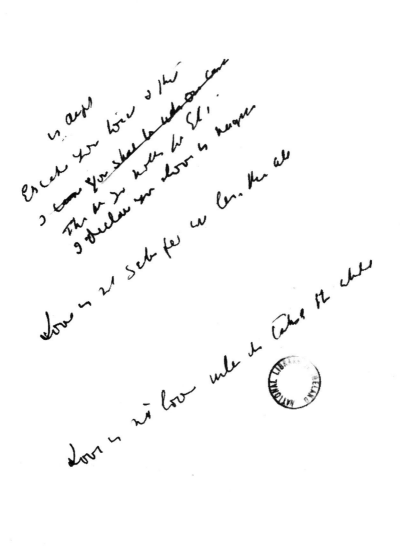

The candle & hidden & it freely should
The curtains drawn on the unfriendly night
That we abscond & yet guns abscond
who to escape then or as or days)

Plate 6: Draft 3.

echoes the great tradition, but has moved from Plato to Shakespeare as model for avoiding impediments to union. "Love is not love unless it takes the whole" is surely a reminiscence of Sonnet 116: "Let me not to the marriage of true minds/Admit impediments. Love is not love/ Which alters when it alteration finds. . ."[19] The Day of Judgment figures in this sonnet—love "bears it out even to the edge of doom"— but has not yet entered Yeats's poem. Shakespeare's sonnet echoes the marriage service. "I require and charge you (as you will answer at the dreadful day of judgment, when the secrets of of all hearts shall be desclosed) that if either of you do know any impediment why ye may not be lawfully joined together in matrimony, that ye confess it."[20] It also echoes I Corinthians 13: "Charity beareth all things" and "never faileth." All, I think, go into the pot which is the matrix of Yeats's poem.

Draft 3, which is on the verso of Draft 1, preserves jottings which try the rhymes "aught," "that" (or "thot"), and "naught" for the content of Stanza 3 of the prose sketch. The five-beat refrains are repeated but in reverse order to give climactic place to the stronger rhyme, "whole".

Draft 3

```
        if[?] aegt [=aught]

  Escape your touch & that [or, thot]

  I o***** You shal be *** out[?] cast[?]

  Th* are you nothing[?] for Etc

  I declare yo[ur] love is naught




  Love is not satisfied with less than all




  Love is not love unless it takes the whole
```

Note: "Out cast" is a probable reading. But I have tried "under our curse" for the same phrase. The reader can speculate as well as I about the undeciphered words. "C****" is possibly an elliptical "caught."

23

The other five-beat line, "Love is not satisfied with less than all," is surely a very relevant, though perhaps unconscious, echo of Item V in Blake's "There Is No Natural Religion" (Second Series). "If the many become the same as the few when possess'd, More! More! is the cry of a mistaken soul; less than All cannot satisfy Man." Other parts are relevant. Jane perceives more than can be discovered by her acute senses: "Man's perceptions are not bounded by organs of perception; he percieves more than sense (tho' ever so acute) can discover" (Item I). Jane seems to be asking the impossible: "If any could desire what he is incapable of possessing, despair must be his eternal lot" (Item VI). Jane's solution is that " 'All could be known or shown/If Time were but gone.' " She longs for an infinite possession: "The desire of Man being Infinite, the possession is Infinite & himself Infinite" (Item VII: *Complete Writings of William Blake,* pp. 97-98).

Drafts 4 — 7 appear much later in the notebook and many of the intervening pages have been cut out, leaving only stubs. It is possible, therefore, that there were other drafts of "Crazy Jane on the Day of Judgment" on some of these pages. I doubt it, however. The number of manuscript pages we have for this poem and the rate of progress in writing the poem accord well with other examples in "Words for Music Perhaps."

Nor can one tell how much time elapsed between the writing of Draft 3 and the writing of Draft 4 because Yeats has jumped around considerably in the notebook. Both Draft 1 and Draft 6 are dated October.

Draft 4 is on a left-hand page, facing Draft 5, and contains version: of Stanzas 1 — 3.

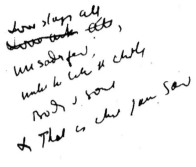

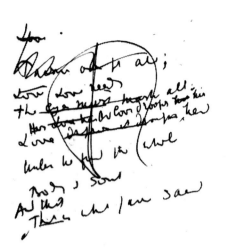

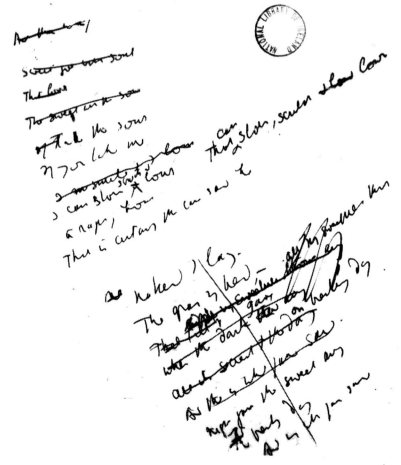

Draft 4

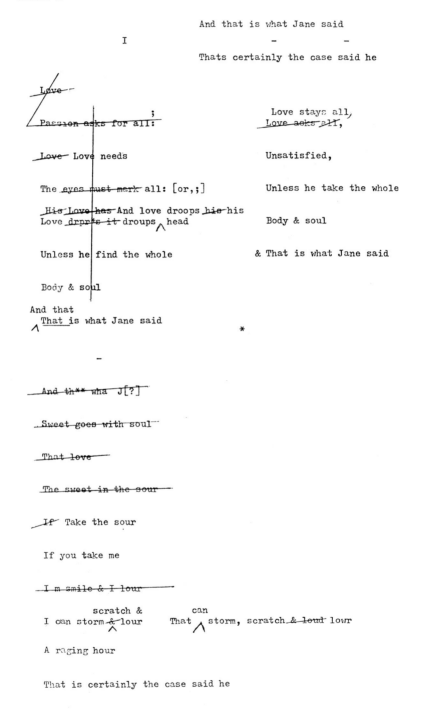

                                        And that is what Jane said
                I   —   —
                                        Thats certainly the case said he

    ~~Love~~ —

    ~~Passion asks for all~~:   ;   Love stays all,
                                                    ~~Love asks all~~,

    ~~Love~~ Love needs   Unsatisfied,

    The ~~eyes must mark~~ all: [or,;]   Unless he take the whole

    ~~His Love has~~ And love droops ~~his~~ his
    Love ~~drprfs it~~ droops ∧ head   Body & soul

    Unless he find the whole   & That is what Jane said

    Body & soul

And that
  ∧ That is what Jane said   *

                    —

    ~~And th** wha~~ J[?]

    ~~Sweet goes with soul~~

    ~~That love~~

    ~~The sweet in the sour~~

    ~~If~~ Take the sour

    If you take me

    ~~I m smile & I lour~~

            scratch &   can
    I can storm & lour   That ∧ storm, scratch & ~~loud~~ lowr
            ∧

    A raging hour

    That is certainly the case said he

                        26

[break]

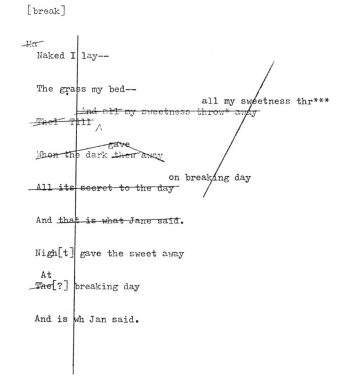

Naked I lay--

The grass my bed--

all my sweetness thr***

~~And all my sweetness throw* away~~

~~Thel Till~~

gave

~~When the dark they away~~

on breaking day

~~All its secret to the day~~

And ~~that is what Jane said.~~

Nigh[t] gave the sweet away

At
~~The~~[?] breaking day

And is wh Jan said.

Yeats has now determined the refrains which make the finished poem a dialogue. "And that is what Jane said" underlines Jane's downright character as well as half seriously making her statements prophetic utterances, worthy of record. " 'That's certainly the case,' said he" subordinates Jack, or the unnamed male, whose tone will change from amused to serious indulgence as Yeats manipulates the context. These refrains establish certain rhymes. Line 2 in Stanzas 1 and 3 will have to rhyme with "said." Line 2 of Stanzas 2 and 4 must rhyme with "he."

As we shall see, the first stanza of the finished poem is ambiguous, and meaningful ambiguity is one device by which Yeats makes these songs irrefutable. In Draft 4 we can see this ambiguity entering Stanza 1. Let us follow the evolution of this stanza. At first Jane states positively that love or passion "asks for all" and can "find" or "take the whole/Body and soul" To find a rhyme for "said" Yeats personifies Eros. The change from "its" to "his" introduces the personification.

```
      Love
    /
  / Passion asks for all:   ;
  /
   Love   Love needs

   The eyes must mark all: [or,;]

   His Love has And love droops his his
   Love drops it droups ^ head

   Unless he find the whole

   Body & soul

 And that
   That is what Jane said
 ^
```

"Unsatisfied" replaces "head," but Love continues to be "he."

```
        Love stays all,
        Love asks all,

        Unsatisfied,

        Unless he take the whole

        Body & soul
```

A transitional step is the revision of "Love asks all,/Unsatisfied," above, to "Love stays all/Unsatisfied."

In the next version of Stanza 1—if we may jump ahead for a moment to Draft 6—the personification is no longer pointed to (though not clearly eliminated) by the revisions. "He" is gone. Thus Yeats avoids distracting the reader from the swift—but now triumphantly ambiguous —sentence he has made of Lines 1—4.

```
                    is
        Love asks all ; [?]

          Un
         Un satisfied

        That cannot
         Until he take the whole

        Body & soul:

        And that is what Jane said
```

Is all love inevitably unsatisfied since no love can ever take the whole? Or can some love take the whole and therefore be satisfied? The ambiguity is deliberate—representing the dilemma of mortal love—and Yeats thought of both alternatives before opting for the ambiguity. At one point Jane declares "Nothing can be shown/True love cannot be."

But let us go on with Draft 4 and its versions of Stanzas 2 and 3. Stanza 2 is a development of the second stanza prose sketch: "Why do you complain that I am not all kind [?]" But in Draft 4 Yeats has found "sweet" and "sour" to express Jane's temperament and perfects the stanza within these terms.

```
        And th** wha J[?]

        Sweet goes with soul

        That love

        The sweet in the sour

        If  Take the sour

        If you take me

        I m smile & I lour

                scratch &              can
        I can storm & lour    That  storm, scratch & loud lowr

        A raging hour

        That is certainly the case said he
```

"Take the sour if you take me" has the advantage of fitting into the language of the marriage service:: "I [Jack] take thee [Jane] to my wedded wife, to have and to hold from this day forward, for better, for worse, for richer, for poorer, in sickness, and in health, to love and to cherish, till death us depart"*(Book of Common Prayer,* p. 292).

The version "I can storm scratch & lour/A raging hour" reminds us that "lour" can mean not only "to frown" but also "to be dark and threatening, as clouds." "Lour" already suggests a darkening of the spiritual weather, and the Draft 4 version of the third stanza, like the third stanza of Draft 1, introduces imagery of night.

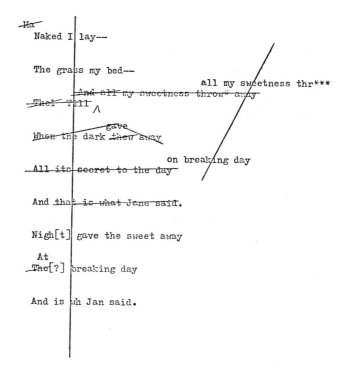

When Yeats tackles this third stanza, he has no trouble with the words "Naked I lay—/The grass my bed—" which are the same, except for punctuation, in the printed texts. The conception has changed from that in the prose sketch: "See ~~th~~ in the night, when we meet in/the dark wood, that you touch all portions of/my body. . . ." Here the meeting has already happened. Instead of asking for perfect physical contact, the poet who wrote "Love's pleasure drives his love away" ("Two Songs from a Play," *Variorum Poems,* p. 438) is asking through Jane for a love which can embrace the whole cycle, sour as well as sweet, day as well as night, satiation as well as desire, and death as well as life. "All flesh is grass" says the Psalm in the burial service, and the two lines can evoke an image of death as well as of love.

For lines 3 and 4 of this third stanza Yeats tried in succession:

Till
And all my sweetness throw[n] away
When the dark th[r]ew away
When the dark gave away
All its secret to the day
All its secret on breaking day
Nigh[t] gave the sweet away
At breaking day.

Jane seems to be sweet by night and sour by day, like the "loathly lady" of the romance in which Gawain must choose whether his bride be fair by night and foul by day or fair by day and foul by night.

Draft 5 is really a continuation of Draft 4 and faces it on the right-hand page. It contains two versions of Stanza 4 and one of Stanza 3.

Draft 5

```
        Mouths thirst on . -


        Until




        ****


        But love thirsts on

        But mouths thirst on




        Lover has for known
      ┌No
      └P    peace can there[?] be

        Till[?] prides day has gone

        And al[?] shown[?]

        Tht [=That's] cerny [=certainly]



    [break]
```

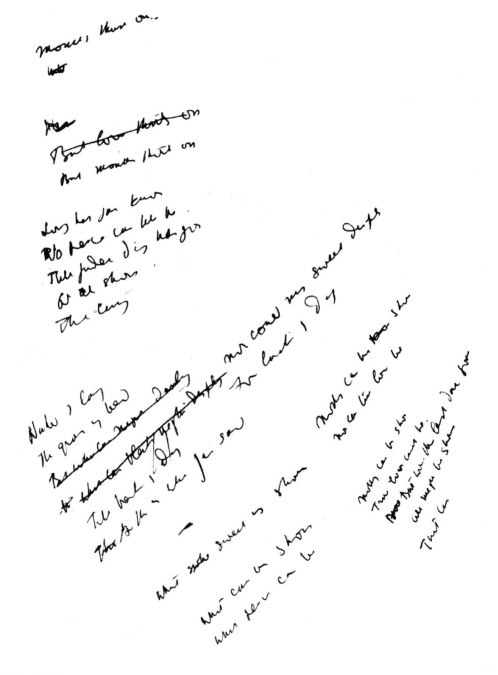

Plate 8: Draft 5.

```
Naked I lay

The grass my bed

But what can night display

                              Nor could my sweet display
* What can black night display
                              For lack of day

Till break of day

Th  And that is what Jane said


              —


                        Nothing can be knew shown

What swhe sweet is shown

                        Nor can true love be



What can be shown

                  Nothing can be shown

What peace can be

                  True love cannot be.

                  Bure But were the last day gone

                  All might be shown

                  That cer
```

To begin with Yeats makes his first attempts at Stanza 4. In spite of the consummation, desire continues, "Mouths thirst on/Until." Until what? Considering the rhyme scheme, perhaps Yeats was leading up to "Till pride's day has gone/And all shown." Rather than introduce a new distracting image, Yeats substitutes for "Mouths thirst on" a general summary statement.

```
Lover has for known

 ⎧No
 ⎨
 ⎩P        peace can there[?] be

     Till[?] prides day has gone

     And al[?] shown[?]

       Tht [=That's] cerny [=certainly]
```

The day-night imagery gets a bit complex with "pride's day." Presumably "pride's day" ends when a night of humiliation, or at least of humility, lays Jane naked on the grass and gives her "sweet" away to the next breaking day. But what is that new day? Unlike "pride's day" it should be the dawn of an immortal love which unites the antinomies: "Until the day break, and the shadows flee away, turn, my beloved. . ." *(Song of Solomon* 2:17).

The remainder of Draft is occupied with a rewriting of Stanzas 3 and 4. Before going on to these revisions, let us stop and reconstruct the poem as it stands at this point in its development, taking the latest versions of lines and eliminating the distracting cancelled items. I have also eliminated the comma at the end of the first line since it is inconsistent with the revision "Love stays all/Unsatisfied" and Yeats later removed it.

> Love stays all
> Unsatisfied,
> Unless he take the whole
> Body & soul
> And that is what Jane said
>
> Take the sour
> If you take me
> That can storm, scratch lowr
> A raging hour
> That is certainly the case said he.
>
> Naked I lay—
> The grass my bed—
> Night gave the sweet away
> At breaking day
> And that is what Jane said.

With "And all shown" we are back to the thought "all must I display" of the first draft. In earlier versions we have looked at, certain lines accord with that thought: "The eyes must mark all," "And love

34

droops his head/Unless he find the whole/Body & soul," "When the dark gave away/All the secret to the day," "Night gave the sweet away/To [or, At?] breaking day." "Gave away" may be used in the sense of "revealed" or "betrayed." Jane is the passive subject of this revealing. Night revealed the "sweet" to day and also yielded the "sweet" to him as beloved to lover, losing it in the process.

Jane longs for the resolving of the antinomies. Though she desires to reveal and yield her sweet, to do so is to lose it. Her daytime self can be sufficiently sour. The trouble with Stanza 3 has been that day becomes both the time of the revelation of the sweet and the time of her being sour.

Turning back to Draft 5 we see that in the revision of Stanza 3 Yeats's logical difficulties with day and night, sweet and sour, are overcome by making night the time when she is sweet but cannot reveal her sweetness, while day is the time when she can reveal herself but is sour.

```
          Naked I lay


          The grass my bed


      But what can night display

                               Nor could my sweet display
      *That can black night display
                               For lack of day

          Till break of day


      Th* And that is what Jane said
```

There has been a change from a passive submission to night to an active attempt to reveal all, to take off not only clothes but all time-bound concealments. More and more the night is becoming a symbol of this mortal life in which one cannot know or show all and the breaking day is becoming a symbol of eternity.

Next Yeats tries another version of Stanza 4. With daylight as revelation, a new idea enters the poem: the end of the world. The stanza is revised to include "the last day."

```
          Nothing can be shown


          True love cannot be.


      Burc But were the last day gone


          All might be shown


          That cer
```

35

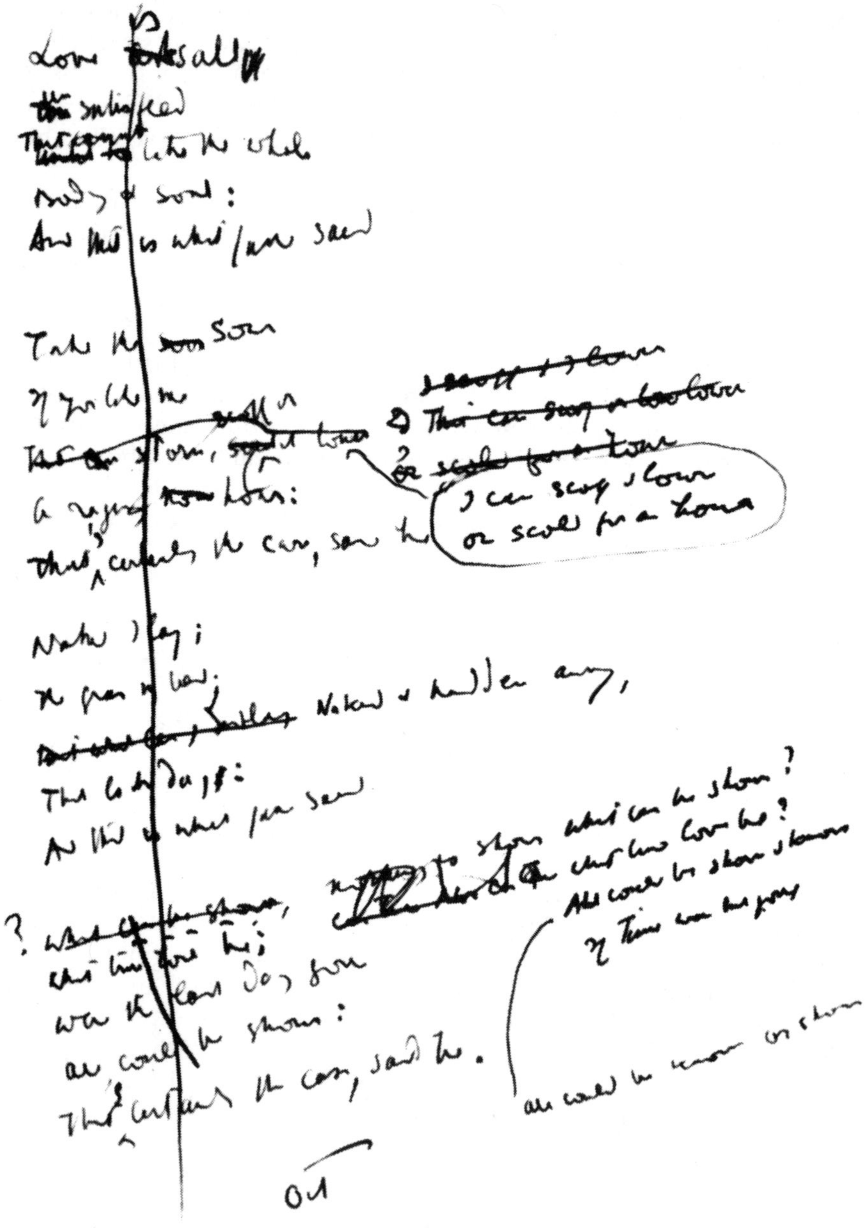

Plate 9: Draft 5.

Draft 6 is on the next right-hand page after Draft 5 and contains revisions of all four stanzas which bring the poem near to its final form.

Draft 6

```
          is
Love  asks all , [?]

   Un
 Un satisfied

That cannot
 Until he take the whole

Body & soul:

And that is what Jane said




                 sour
Take the sour

If you take me                        I scoff & I lower

              scoff or
That can storm, scratch, lower    I   That can scoff[?] or low lower
                      ∧
                                      I
A raging ho** hour:               or scold for an hour

    's                            ┌─────────────────────────┐
That   certainly the case, said he│ I can scoff & lowr      │
     ∧                            │                         │
                                  │ or scold for a[n] hour  │
                                  └─────────────────────────┘


Naked I lay;

The grass my bed;

But what can I display Naked & hidden away,

That lack day  :

And that is what Jane said.

[break]
```

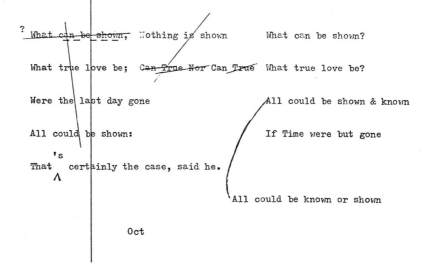

```
?
 What can be shown,   Nothing is shown      What can be shown?

 What true love be;   Can True Nor Can True  What true love be?

 Were the last day gone                     All could be shown & known

 All could be shown:                         If Time were but gone
        's
 That    certainly the case, said he.
       ^
                                            All could be known or shown

              Oct
```

We have already discussed the evolution of Stanza 1. Stanza 2 is not changed in concept though it is simplified and perfected. It is in Stanzas 3 and 4 that Yeats solves the imagery problems which vexed Draft 5. "Day" cannot stand for both Time ("Were the last day gone")·and Eternity ("break of day"). First the "day" image is confirmed in a revision of Stanza 3.

```
Naked I lay;

The grass my bed;

But what can I display  Naked & hidden away,

That lack day :

And that is what Jane said.
```

Then Stanza 4 is revised to eliminate the word "day," substituting "Time":

```
What can be shown?

What true love be?

All could be shown & known

    If Time were but gone




All could be known or shown
```

To go back for a moment to Stanza 3, the change from "But what can I display" to "Naked and hidden away" may be an escape from a too obvious Blakean echo, and the Blakean context may have something to do with the Last Day's entering the poem. In his notes to "The Laocoon," which Yeats often quotes, Blake declares "Art can never exist without Naked Beauty displayed" (*Complete Writings,* p. 776). ". . .Beauty," says Yeats writing on Blake, is "the one mask through which can be seen the unveiled eyes of eternity." Love, therefore, along with old age and death, is "first among the arts." "True art is the flame of the Last Day, which begins for every man when he is first moved by beauty, and which seeks to burn all things until they become 'infinite and holy.' "[21] One thinks again of "The Whirlwind of Lovers." Blake shows Paolo and Francesca as much more obviously draped when he depicts them in the flame, but in the sun they seem nearly naked.

At any rate, Crazy Jane, in this third stanza, is struggling and failing to live up to Blake's adage: "Art [and love is 'first among the arts'] can never exist without Naked Beauty displayed."

> Naked I lay;
> The grass my bed;
> But what can I display
> That lack day. . .

Draft 7, on the next right-hand page after Draft 6, is essentially a fair copy of the latter. This draft is of great interest because for the first time since Draft 1 the poem has a title.

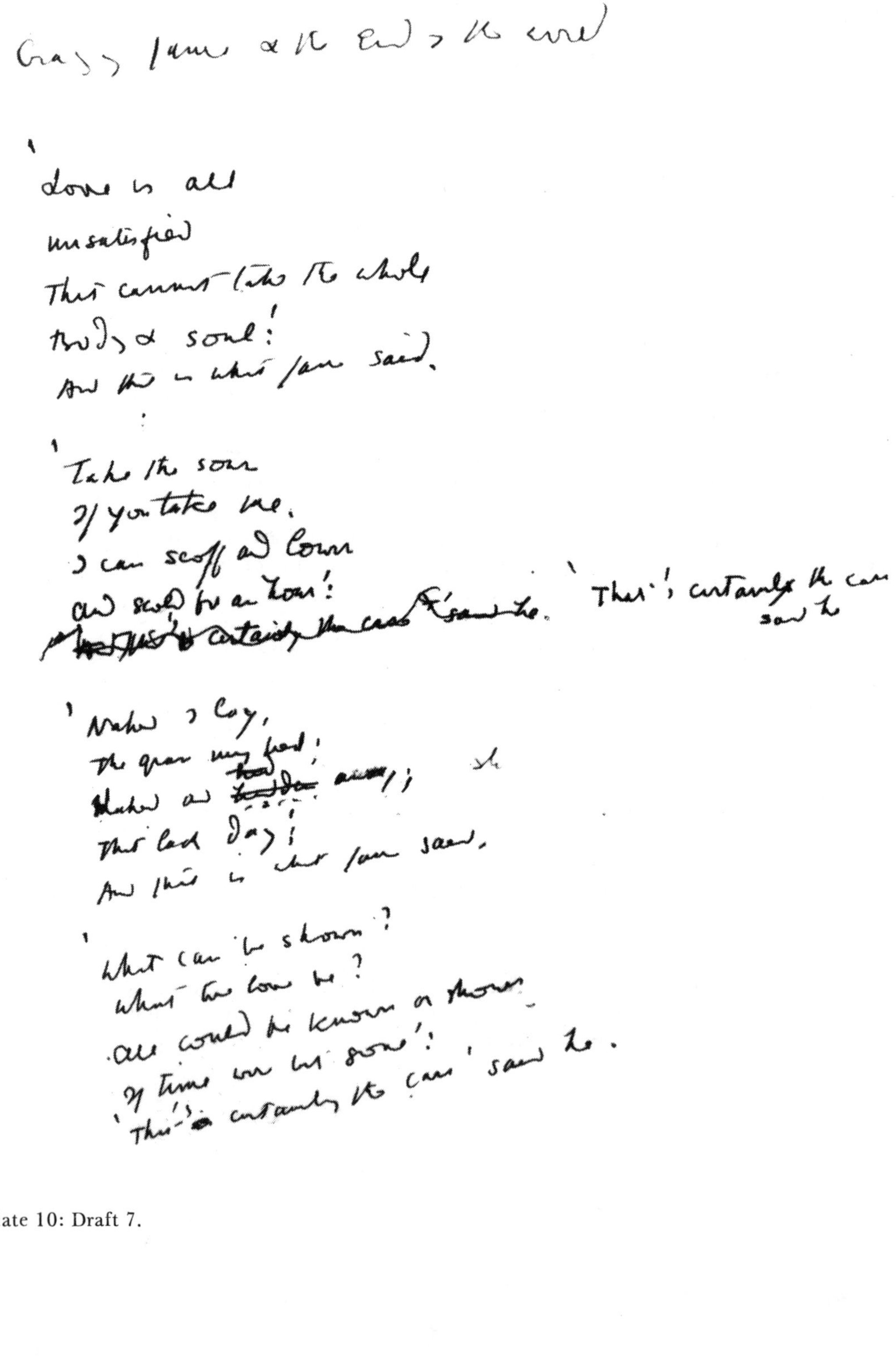

Grass James of the End of the end

'
'love is all
unsatisfied
That cannot take the whole
body & soul!
And this is what James said.

'Take the sour
If you take me.
I can scoff and louus
and scold for an hour!'
'This is certainly the case' said he.   'That's certainly the case
                                              said he

'Nature I say,
The grass my friend;
Shaken and faded away;;   sh
That last Day!
And this is what James said.

'What can be shown?
What true love be?
All could be known or shown,
If time were but gone!'
'This's certainly the case' said he.

Plate 10: Draft 7.

Draft 7

Crazy Jane & the End of the World

'Love is all

Unsatisfied

That cannot take the whole

Body & soul':

And that is what Jane said.

'Take the sour

If you take me,

I can scoff and lowr

And scold for an hour':

✗ 'And that is certainly the case' said he. 'That's certainly the case'

said he

'Naked I lay,

The grass my bed;

naked and hidden away;   stet

That lack day':

And that is what Jane said.

'What can be shown?

What true love be?

All could be known or shown

If Time were but gone':

'That is certainly the case' said he.

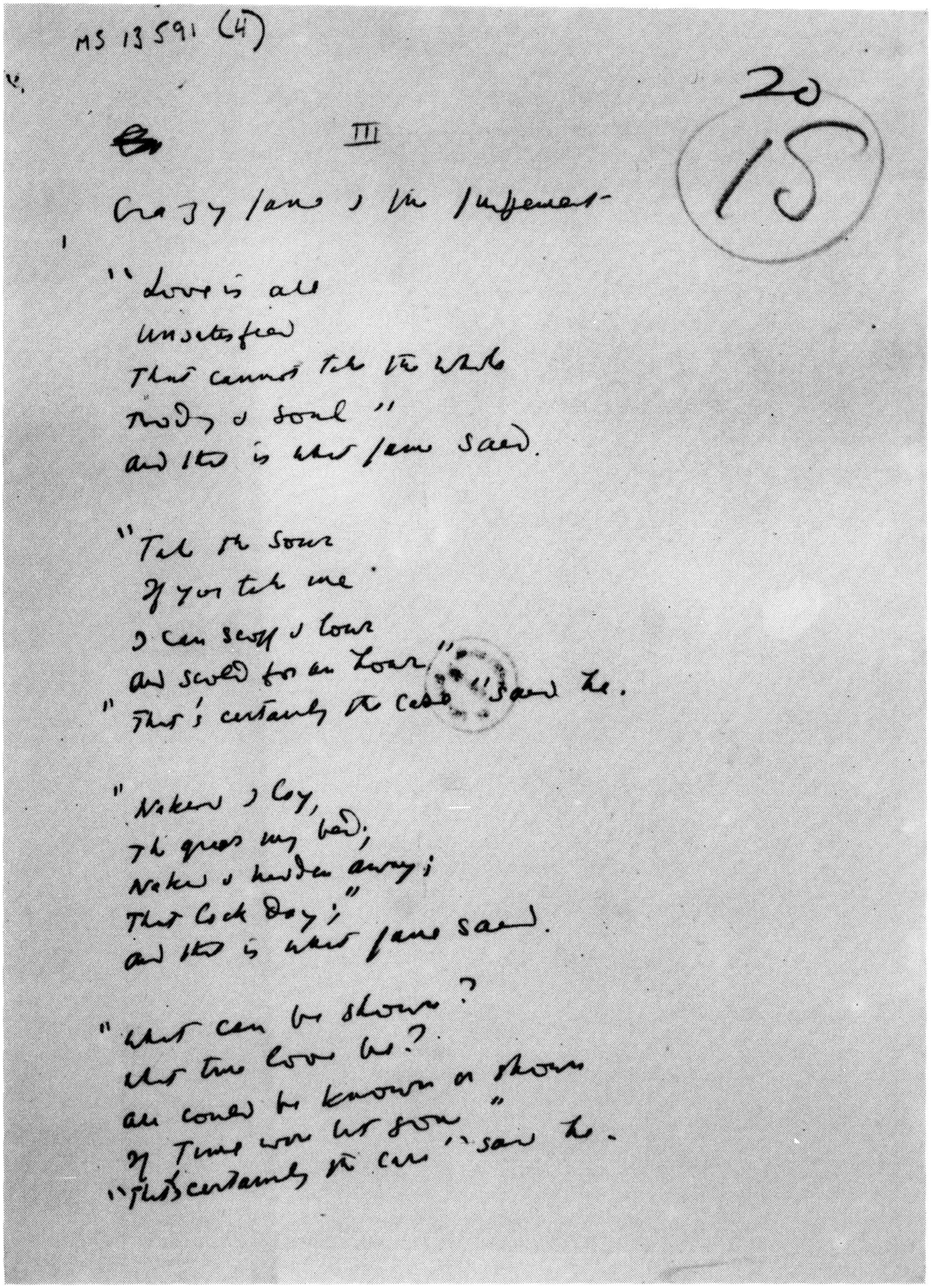

III

Crazy Jane & the Judgement

"Love is all
Unsatisfied
That cannot take the whole
Body & soul"
And that is what Jane said.

"Take the soul
If you take me
I can scoff & lour
And scold for an hour"
"That's certainly the case" said he.

"Naked I lay,
The grass my bed;
Naked & hidden away;
That God day;"
And that is what Jane said.

"What can be shown?
What true love be?
All could be known or shown
If Time were but gone"
"That's certainly the case" said he.

Plate 11: Draft 8.

Note that the word "day"—as in "last day" or "Judgment Day"—is not used, perhaps avoided because of Yeats's earlier trouble with day and night imagery. There is no ambiguity in this title.

Draft 8 is not in the notebook but is on a loose sheet. It was one of a group of fair copies in Yeats's hand of the "Words for Music Perhaps" poems.

Draft 8

20

(18)

~~of~~   III

Crazy Jane & the Judgement

"Love is all

Unsatisfied

That cannot take the whole

Body & soul"

And that is what Jane said.

"Take the sour

If you take me

I can scoff & lour

And scold for an hour"

"That's certainly the case" said he.

[break]

```
"Naked I lay,

The grass my bed;

Naked & hidden away;

That lack day;"

And that is what Jane said.




"What can be shown?

What true love be?

All could be known or shown

If Time were but gone"

"That's certainly the case" said he.
```

The special interest of this draft is the title: "Crazy Jane & the Judgment." Once again the word "day" is avoided, but here the avoidance seems calculated to introduce an ambiguity. "Judgment Day" could have meant only one thing, but "the Judgment" could be any judgment. After all, Jane is trying to show what can be shown and Jack is deciding whether to take her or not, which is a judgment. "In the beginning of love. . .," says Yeats, "there is a moment when we understand more perfectly than we understand again until all is finished" (*Essays and Introductions*, p. 111).[22]

Typescripts were made from the fair copies of the poems in "Words for Music Perhaps," but I have not found the typescript for this poem. Nor have I been able to find the proofs of the first printing (Cuala Press, 1932). Therefore we now move to the first printing itself.

CRAZY JANE ON THE DAY OF JUDGEMENT

'Love is all
Unsatisfied
That cannot take the whole
Body and soul'.

And that is what Jane said.

44

'Take the sour
If you take me;
I can scoff and lour
And scold for an hour'.

'That's certainly the case' said he.

'Naked I lay
The grass my bed;
Naked and hidden away
That black day;'

And that is what Jane said.

'What can be shown?
What true love be?
All could be known or shown
If Time were but gone'.

'That's certainly the case' said he.

The more I leave the door unlatched
The sooner love is gone,
For love is but a skein unwound
Between the dark and dawn.

A lonely ghost the ghost is
That to God shall come;
I, love's skein upon the ground
My body in the tomb,
Shall leap into the light lost
In my mother's womb.

But were I left to lie alone
In an empty bed——
The skein so bound us ghost to ghost
When you turned your head
Passing on the road that night——
Mine would walk, being dead.

CRAZY JANE ON THE DAY
OF JUDGEMENT
'Love is all
Unsatisfied
That cannot take the whole
Body and soul'.

And that is what Jane said.

26

'Take the sour
If you take me;
I can scoff and lour
And scold for an hour'.

'That's certainly the case' said he.

'Naked I lay
The grass my bed;
Naked and hidden away
That black day;'

And that is what Jane said.

'What can be shown?
What true love be?
All could be known or shown
If Time were but gone'.

'That's certainly the case' said he.

CRAZY JANE ON GOD
That lover of a night
Came when he would,
Went in the dawning light

27

Except for punctuation, this printing differs at only two points from the fair copy, Draft 8. There is a new title, "Crazy Jane on the Day of Judgement." Note that "Day of Judgement" preserves the ambiguity which we said "Judgment Day" would destroy. Any day can be a day of judgment, small "j", but there is only the Judgment Day. The substitution of "on" for "and" introduces another possible meaning: "Crazy Jane Discourses upon the Day of Judgment" (Longinus "On the Sublime," Crazy Jane "On the Day of Judgment). Note too that Yeats has chosen the phrase which occurs in the marriage service: "the dreadful day of judgment when the secrets of all hearts shall be disclosed".

The second change which occurs in the first printing is the change of "That lack day" to "That black day." I would wager that if the missing typescripts and proofs are found they will show that these two revisions were made simultaneously and depend upon each other. Some of the ambiguities in the title are also in "That black day," for the Judgment Day is a black day, and, since it is the ushering in of Eternity, it has in a sense already happened. Previous to this simple change, the addition of a "b", the third stanza can refer only to Jane's unsuccessful—because time-bound—attempt to display all to Jack during a night of love.

> Naked I lay,
> The grass my bed;
> Naked & hidden away;
> That lack day. . .

With the placing of a "b" before the "l" of "lack," the stanza resonates from the Creation to the Judgment Day.

It may have been the syntax of Stanza 3 that made Yeats revise it. "A powerful and passionate syntax" *(Essays and Introductions*, p. 522) was what he sought. Syntax could be intricate, even rhetorical, if dramatically effective, that is, natural considering the speaker, the situation and the emotion expressed. The syntax is natural enough in

> Naked I lay;
> The grass my bed;
> But what can I display
> That lack day. . . .

Not liking the repetition of "I", perhaps, and liking the paradox of "Naked and hidden away", he cancels "But what can I display." By so doing he loses the second "I", the nearby and natural referent for "That". Immediately the syntax becomes very strained, stiff, and unnatural, "That" having to refer way back up to the "I" in Line 1. The need for a natural vigorous syntax created a pressure to change "lack" from a verb to an adjective.

The addition of a "b" before "lack" accomplished that change, and the phrase is good Anglo-Irish idiom: "A bad black day."[23] The change creates almost no alteration in sound pattern. But what an alteration in richness of statement! The metaphor by which night equals Time, day Eternity, is abandoned. "That black day" is in the past. "Naked I lay" on "that black day." A black day on which the redoubtable Jane lay defenseless on the grass, "Naked and hidden away", suggests many possibilities. Was Jane alone or with a companion on that black day? There is nothing in Stanza 3 to suggest a companion. But the fourth stanza suggests that she was naked in order to exhibit herself to a lover. The black day fits in to the implied love story of Jack and Jane as the day on which she lost her virginity to Jack.

If the "black day" is to communicate the intensity of the sexual ecstasy shared with Jack, it may have physiological base in the blacking out, the brief moment of unconsciousness, experienced in orgasm. In "Crazy Jane Reproved" Yeats speaks of the "storm that blots the day" in connection with Zeus's rape of Europa.

When Yeats speaks of experience so intense that it leaves the body behind and becomes spiritual experience, he sometimes symbolizes it by a blacking out: "Black out; Heaven blazing into the head" ("Lapis Lazuli," *Variorum Poems,* p. 566); "the sun's/Under eclipse and the day blotted out" ("The Tower," *Variorum Poems,* p. 414). "Donne. . . was never tempted to linger, or rather, to pretend that we can linger, between spirit and sense," wrote Yeats in 1922. "How often had I heard men of my time talk of the meeting of spirit and sense, yet there is no meeting but only change upon the instant, and it is by the perception of a change, like the sudden 'blacking out' of the lights of the stage, that passion creates its most violent sensation" (*Autobiography,* p. 218)

The Day of Judgment too is a black day, and though Jane's black day is in the past and the Day of Judgment is comming in the future, one cannot help remembering that on that day St. Mark prophesies, "the sun shall be darkened" (XIII:24). In the vision of the Judgment in the Revelation of St. John "the sun became black as sackcloth of hair" (Rev. VI:12).

Are these echoes relevant? Sexual union, in the Yeatsian system, is a microcosmic imitation of the end of the world, the Day of Judgment. In *The Only Jealousy of Emer* (1919), the Woman of the Sidhe, seducing Cuchulain, says

> Time shall seem to stay his course;
> When your mouth and my mouth meet.[24]

The natural union of man and woman is "a symbol of that eternal instant where the antinomy is resolved" (*A Vision,* 1937, p. 214. Cf. also pp. 67-69).

47

When in "Solomon and the Witch" (1921) the Queen of Sheba lay like Jane "On grassy mattress. . ./Within [her] arms great Solomon," a supernatural cockerel crowed through her voice. Misled by their sexual ecstasy, the cockerel

> thought,
> Chance being at one with Choice at last,
> All that the brigand apple brought
> And this foul world were dead at last.
> He that crowed out eternity
> Thought to have crowed it in again.

For "the world ends when these two things [Chance and Choice],/ Though several, are a single light. . ." (*Variorum Poems,* p. 388).

Sexual union then simulates the end of the world, the end of time. But because it is only simulation and not the real thing, love is unsatisfied, even in nakedness we are still hidden, the day is black, we cannot be fully known or shown to the lover. "The tragedy of sexual intercourse" Yeats said, "is the perpetual virginity of the souls.[25] Only in death do "the ringers in the tower" appoint "for the hymen of the soul a passing bell" (*Mythologies,* p. 332).

There are other Biblical associations. The Creation: When "darkness was upon the face of the deep" (Gen. 1:2); "And they were both naked, the man and his wife, and were not ashamed" (Gen. II:25). Birth: Job's words, "Let the day perish wherein I was born. . .Let that day of darkness. . .let the blackness of the day terrify it" (III:3-5). The Fall of Man: ". . .They knew that they were naked. . . and Adam and his wife hid themselves from the presence of the Lord God amongst the trees of the garden" (Gen. III:7-8). That was a black day for all. Jane's "Take the sour if you take me" becomes an allusion to the sour, the brigand apple. "Naked and hidden away" suddenly recalls Adam's explanation to God, "I was afraid, because I was naked; and I hid myself" (III:10). The Fall is associated with sex. Milton has Adam and Eve make love immediately after eating the fruit; afterwards they know their nakedness and are ashamed; "thir Eyes how op'n'd, and their minds/How dark'n'd" (*Paradise Lost* IX:1053-54), naked on that black day.

Finally, "The black day" may recall the "through a glass darkly" phrase in St. Paul's great epistle on love in First Corinthians 13, at least in idea, and sometimes even in verbal echoes. Has St. Paul been in the background all the time along with Shakespeare and Plato? Sonnet 116 echoes Corinthians, St. Paul echoes Plato. Yeats perhaps echoes them all. "Love is for wholes," the original refrain, harks back to St. Paul's "when that which is perfect is come, that which is in part shall be done away." In the very first draft of Stanza 1 Jane wants Jack to tell her about when he was a child, spake like a child, and understood as a child. She wants to know every "childes love or hate or indignity" which Jack has put away on becoming a man. Stanza 2, also, echoes Corinthians: Charity "is kind," but Jane admits that she is "not always kind" (Draft 1). Jane's challenge to Jack to "Take the sour/If you take me" asks even more of love than that it suffer long, be kind, and endure all things. Jack has to like it, as well.

In the third stanza of the first draft Jane asks to be fully "known" in a sexual sense. The third stanza of later drafts is full of the limitations of mortal sight: "But what can I display/That lack day."

Stanza 4 has in every draft echoed Corinthians in idea if not in sound: "Charity vaunteth not itself, is not puffed up." "Loving has foreknown/No peace can there be/Till pride's day has gone/And all shown" (Draft 5). The first two lines of the final version—"What can be shown?/What true love be?"—are the very subject of I Corinthians 13. With the addition of the word "known" in Draft 6—"All could be known or shown/If Time were but gone"—and the final addition in Stanza 3 of "That black day" which prevents showing and knowing, the echoes of Corinthians begin quietly to control our responses to the poem:

"For we know in part, and we prophesy in part. But when that which is perfect is come, then that which is in part shall be done away. . . . For now we see through a glass, darkly; but then face to face: now I know in part; but then shall I know even as also I am known."

Yeats said that a poem reached its final form with a click like the closing of a box. I think that click was heard in this case when he added the "b" to "lack", changing a predictable idea to unpredictable imaginative vision. Yet that vision is traditional.

"Talk to me of originality and I will turn on you with rage," he wrote in 1937 (*Essays and Introductions,* p. 522). The working drafts of "Crazy Jane on the Day of Judgment" show Yeats making the tradition his own, turning verse into resonant poetry, irrefutable song.

NOTES

1. *The Autobiography of W. B. Yeats* (New York, 1974), p. 332.
2. *The Complete Writings of William Blake*, ed. Geoffrey Keynes (London, 1966), p. 149.
3. *The Letters of W. B. Yeats*, ed. Allan Wade (London, 1954), p. 922.
4. *The Variorum Edition of the Poems of W. B. Yeats*, ed. Peter Allt and Russell K. Alspach (New York, 1957), p. 510.
5. *The Dialogues of Plato*, trans. B. Jowett, in 4 vols. (Oxford, 1953), I, 524, 521-22.
6. Stephen R. Winnett, *An Edition of the Manuscripts of Two Plays by W. B. Yeats, "The Only Jealousy of Emer" and "Fighting the Waves"* (Oxford University, 1977; unpublished dissertation), pp. 144-45. I have turned Winnett's diplomatic transcriptions into a reading text.
7. William Butler Yeats, *A Vision* (London, 1925), p. 149.
8. W. B. Yeats, *A Vision* (New York, 1937), p. 193.
9. W. B. Yeats, *Memoirs*, ed. Denis Donoghue (London, 1972), p. 128.
10. Donald Torchiana, " 'Among School Children' and the Education of the Irish Spirit," pp. 123-50, *In Excited Reverie*, ed. A. Norman Jeffares and K. G. W. Cross (New York, 1965), p. 139.
11. *The Poetical Works of Dryden*, ed. (rev. and enl.) George R. Noyes (Boston, 1950), pp. 188-189.
12. *The Poems of John Milton*, ed. Helen Darbishire (London, 1961), pp. 288-89
13. W. B. Yeats, *Mythologies* (New York, 1974), p. 356.
14. *The Poems of William Blake*, ed. W. B. Yeats (London, New York, 1893), p. xlv.
15. *Blake's Grave: A Prophetic Book*, with a commentary by S. Foster Damon (Providence, 1963), Plate X.
16. From Damon's commentary, unpaginated.
17. Albert S. Roe, *Blake's Illustrations to the Divine Comedy* (Princeton, 1953), p. 65.
18. The manuscripts of "Crazy Jane on the Day of Judgment" may be found in the National Library of Ireland, Manuscripts 13,581 and 13,591(4). NLMs. 13,581 is a notebook 30cm. x 22cm with a patterned paper cover, blue and white on greenish-tan. It contained five signatures of rather heavy unlined white paper with no watermarks. Folios 1-20 comprise Signature 1, but Folios 8 and 9 have been cut out leaving narrow stubs; Folios 21-40 comprise Signature 2, but Folio 33 is cut out; Folios 41-60 comprise Signature 3, but all have been cut out except Folio 41; all of Signature 4, presumably Folios 61-80, have been cut out; Folios 81-98 comprise Signature 5, but Folios 81-83 are cut out. Many of the stubs have ink marks, so that many of the cut out pages contained writing. Draft 1 of "Crazy Jane on the Day of Judgment" is Folio 39 Recto of the notebook. Draft 2 is Folio 38 Verso, and Draft 3 is Folio 39V. Draft 4 is Folio 90V, Draft 5 is Folio 91R, Draft 6 is Folio 92R, and Draft 7 is Folio 93R. Drafts 1-7 are written in the same grey-black ink, except that in Draft 6 the final versions of Stanza 2, lines 3-4, and all of the final version of Stanza 4 except "All could be known or shown" are in black ink.

    NLMs.13,591(4) contains a (misplaced) letter to Olivia Shakespear, postmark Nov. 23, 1931, and one folio of "Crazy Jane on the Day of Judgment." This folio is white typing paper 25.4cm. x 20.35cm with watermark "Swift Brook Bond." The poem is in blue ink, the Roman numeral III and the number 18 in grey pencil.

Since most of Yeats's manuscripts are now reproduced on microfilm and in bound volumes at the William Butler Yeats Archives, State University of New York at Stony Brook, it is convenient to identify each manuscript page by microfilm reel, bound volume and page. The location of Draft 1 is reel 29, bound volume 7, page 281. The Stony Brook number, therefore, is SB29(7p281). Draft 2 is SB29(7p280); Draft 3 is SB29(7p282); Draft 4 is SB29(8p 16); Draft 5 is SB29(8p 17); Draft 6 is SB29(8p 19); Draft 7 is SB29(8p21); Draft 8 is SB30(3p191).

19   *Shakespeare's Sonnets* (Stratford-on-Avon, 1905).

20   *The Book of Common Prayer, 1559; The Elizabethan Prayer Book*, John E. Booty (Charlottesville, 1976), p. 291.

21. W. B. Yeats, *Essays and Introductions* (New York, 1973), pp. 139-40.

22. Cf. *Beltaine*, 2 (February 1900), pp. 22-23: ". . .As lovers understand in their first glance all that is to befall them, and as poets and musicians see the whole work in its first impulse, so races prophesy at their awakening whatever the generations that are to prolong their traditions shall accomplish in detail. . . If one studies one's own mind, one comes to think with Blake, that 'every time less than a pulsation of the artery is equal to 6000 years, for in this period the poet's work is done; and all the great events of time start forth and are conceived in such a period, within a pulsation of the artery.' "

23. The phrase occurs in a noted passage of Martin Doul's unsuccessful wooing of Molly Byrne in J. M. Synge's *The Well of the Saints:* ". . . A bad black day when I was roused up and found I was the like of the little children do be listening to the stories of an old woman, and do be dreaming after in the dark night that it's in grand houses of gold they are, with speckled horses to ride, and do be waking again, in a short while, and they destroyed with the cold, and the thatch dripping, maybe, and the starved ass braying in the yard." *The Plays and Poems of J. M. Synge*, ed. T. R. Henn (London, 1963), pp. 152-53. Cf. also the "black hags," the "black knot," and "the pig with the black feet" in *Riders to the Sea*.

24. *The Variorum Edition of the Plays of W. B. Yeats*, ed. Russell K. Alspach, assisted by Catharine C. Alspach (New York, 1966), p. 555.

25. Sir William Rothenstein, *Since Fifty* (London, 1939), p. 242; quoted by George Brandon Saul, *Prolegomena to the Study of Yeats's Poems* (Philadelphia, 1957), p. 147.

ILLUSTRATIONS

ACKNOWLEDGMENTS

All unpublished manuscripts by W. B. Yeats are copyright c 1978 by Anne Yeats and Michael Butler Yeats. Thanks are due to them, to the Macmillan Company, New York, to Macmillan & Company Ltd., London, and to the trustees of the National Library of Ireland for permission to publish. The cooperation of A. P. Watt & Son is acknowledged. My work on Yeats manuscripts has been done partly in the homes of the late Mrs. W. B. Yeats, of Senator and Mrs. Michael Yeats, and of Miss Anne Yeats, and I thank them for their hospitality and help. Thanks are due similarly to Director Alf MacLochlainn and the staff of the National Library. Much preliminary transcription was done conveniently in the United States from the microfilms at the new William Butler Yeats Archives of the State University of New York at Stony Brook, and I thank Director Lewis Lusardi and Mr. Narayan Hegde for many favors. I should also thank Miriam and David Finklestein and Richard and Felice Levine for hospitality in Stony Brook. My recent work in Ireland was supported by grants from the American Philosophical Society, the American Council of Learned Societies, and the National Endowment for the Humanities. I thank the Jack Nielsens of Clondalkin for welcoming me into their home for the duration of my stay in Ireland. Part of my work was done at the University of Cambridge, and I thank President John Morrison of Wolfson College, where I was a Visiting Fellow. I thank the University of Massachusetts for a sabbatical leave in 1978 and for the help of its Library staff and Audio-visual Department and my students there for their criticisms and suggestions. I thank my wife, who typed and criticized, and my daughter Rosalind who was my research assistant.

This essay began as a lecture for the English Department at Syracuse University, and I thank my friend Arthur Hoffman, then chairman, for asking me to give it. A somewhat shorter version of the essay has appeared in *The Malahat Review*.